SUZANNE KASLER
TIMELESS STYLE

It is all about style

[signature]

2015.

SUZANNE KASLER
TIMELESS STYLE

WRITTEN WITH CHRISTINE PITTEL, DESIGNED BY DOUG TURSHEN WITH DAVID HUANG

Rizzoli
NEW YORK

New York Paris London Milan

To John and Alexandra

Introduction

Style is elusive—easy to recognize but hard to pin down. It's a way of expressing yourself and it can take many different forms—fashion, art, architecture, and design. I'm inspired by anything visual, especially fashion. Whenever I'm in a new city, I'll stop by the Prada boutique, just to see what Miuccia Prada is thinking about. Her clothes always have an edge. I'm also addicted to Chanel, where Karl Lagerfeld keeps reinventing the classics. Then there's Chloé . . . Céline . . . and Alber Elbaz at Lanvin, who said something recently that stayed with me. He explained that he's not interested in trends. He just wants to make beautiful clothes.

I just want to make beautiful interiors. And I'm not offended when people call my work pretty. I like things to be pretty. I want to give the eye a treat. But that doesn't mean that everything in a room has to be museum quality. The real fun, for me, comes with mixing high and low. I love fine antiques, but I'll often combine them with pieces I've picked from a catalog or something as simple as stones found on a beach. Unexpected juxtapositions are part of my style.

Inspiration is everywhere, if you know how to look. Keep your eyes open, as we do instinctively when we travel. In Paris, I treat the streets like a museum. I look in shop windows. Could anything be quite so tempting as the macarons at Ladurée, in the most luscious pastels? It seems almost a sacrilege to eat them. At Goyard, a luggage store that's been around since 1853, I'm charmed by the way they stack a tower of trunks on the sidewalk.

Sometimes the simplest things give me great pleasure. I can spend hours at La Mercerie Parisienne, a store devoted to ribbon. I'll have them cut yard after yard for me in all sorts of colors. Then when I get home to Atlanta, I will spread them out on my bed and start playing with various combinations. I've worked out some of my most interesting palettes that way.

When I'm designing a house for new clients, one of the best parts of the process is helping them discover their own style as we shop together and gradually develop the concept. I don't believe in merely presenting people with a finished product. I prefer to work together to create a house that reflects not only how they live but also who they are.

In this book, I'll take you through eight houses, including my own, and you'll see how different people and places inspired me. The rooms are filled with things that have meaning to each client because that personal touch is what gives a house its soul. Anything can be the catalyst. One year, I was planning a trip to Paris and was thrilled to be invited to all the fashion shows. The invitations alone were so elegant, with my name written in various styles of calligraphy, that I kept each one. When I came home, I decided to frame them. Now they're hanging in my dressing room and every time I pass by, I'm reminded of all that excitement and creativity. Those bits of paper give me just as much pleasure as the most valuable antique.

So find what you love and surround yourself with it. Live with it. That, to me, is the definition of timeless style.

MOLYNEUX
LOUIS VUITTON
SALADINO VILLA

AT HOME

I have a roving eye—for houses, not for men, I should explain. My husband, John Morris, and I have been married for years and we were happily ensconced in our home in Atlanta with our daughter, Alexandra, when I started to get restless. And I know why. That house was completely done. There were no more rooms to furnish, no new objects to arrange, no problems left to solve. That's when I found myself driving down unfamiliar streets on my way home from work, looking for "For Sale" signs.

I told John I needed a shorter commute and wanted to live in an older neighborhood—both true—but what I really longed for was a blank canvas. There's always some new idea I want to try. In my own house, I can experiment in a way that I can't necessarily do when I'm designing for other people. And then if a client has a hard time visualizing a particular finish or a curtain trim, I could just run them over to my house and show them, if I lived close by. (See how easy it is to rationalize!)

We narrowed the search down to one particular street in Buckhead, with big, shady trees and fine, old houses. I fell in love with one, but then we lost it in a bidding war. I was very upset, and some time went by before I came back to take another look at a Federal-style house I had dismissed earlier. Built in the 1930s, it was basically a red brick box. Someone had modernized the interior and done an addition on the

An entryway will feel more welcoming if you create a place to sit. The antique French bench also provides a convenient spot to drop a coat or a bag. I chose the gray silk and the Fortuny fabric on the pillows for their mercurial sheen. The bench echoes the tones of the mirror and the rim on the table, pulling the three pieces into an integrated composition.

PREVIOUS SPREAD: Architect William T. Baker designed a new, more imposing entrance—a limestone portico supported by Doric columns—and added limestone lintels to accentuate the French doors. We painted the red brick a soft cream, basically to white it out. Do you see the bull's-eye window with its distinctive mullion in the center of the pediment? That became a signature detail that we carried throughout the house. I thought the landscaping should be as architectural as the house. Made up primarily of boxwoods in strong, simple shapes, it has a European look.

RIGHT: In the entryway, we laid Bulgarian white limestone on the floor and painted the stair rail and the baseboards black to create a defining line around the perimeter. A pedestal table made out of burl wood anchors the space and has that 1940s French look, just like the parchment bench. The French lantern is actually a 1940s original. I thought the shape was great, and it inspired me to do my own version for Visual Comfort. The geometric watercolors are by the Russian Suprematist painter Ivan Kliun.

back. And what happened to all those Federal ideals of symmetry? Even the front door was off-center. But here's something to keep in mind when you're looking at a house: If the location and the price are right, you can change the details. And if you want to go even further, you can completely transform its character.

I stood on the front lawn and stared at the house. I had to admit it was a great site—on a hilltop. And I realized that I could give the place a whole new look by reconfiguring the addition, expanding the footprint, moving the front door to the center of a reworked facade, and replacing the first-floor windows with gracious French doors. Suddenly, I was excited. Maybe I could actually turn this into a Regency-style house, the kind I've always wanted—glamorous and dressy but still somehow simple and clean.

My furniture is eclectic, and in this house it all looks comfortably at home. When I fall in love with a piece, I don't worry about period or provenance because I think a room is infinitely more interesting when you mix things up. Here, what holds it all together is a cool, soothing background in shades of white, ecru, and cream. Then, as you walk through the house, accent colors emerge and unfold. The same blue and taupe that's in the living room rug reappears on the curtains and the wallpaper in the dining room and on the ceiling in the family room, where a burst of orange adds another note. I've found that you can use lots of different colors in the same house if they all have the same value—landing at a similar point on the scale of light to dark.

I had such freedom on this project because architect William T. Baker and I reshaped the space to my taste and added details that we chose. And I was my own client, which meant I could decorate every room in exactly the way I wanted.

This is probably not how most people would hang a group of antique miniatures. But look at the angle the staircase creates and the similarly angled shapes in that Clarence House fabric, Velours Klee, on my Laurent dining chair for Hickory Chair. The pattern reminds me of the Russian Constructivists, so I hung the miniatures in an unexpected way that creates its own shape. I love symmetry, but sometimes asymmetry can be more intriguing.

Here's a very simple lesson that I learned early on: if you group like objects instead of scattering them around a room, they will have more impact. These prints, by the American artist Kris Ruhs, are hung in a tight grid to magnify their graphic punch.

OPPOSITE: One of my favorite stores in the world is 10 Corso Como in Milan, and that's where John and I found the prints that are now hanging over my living room sofa. They were in a book that was meant to be taken apart. It's interesting how a series of small pieces can give you the power of a large painting—without a large price tag. I wanted a sofa with long, lean lines and no arms so I designed it myself, for Hickory Chair. Covered in creamy silk velvet by John Saladino and adorned with Fortuny pillows, it looks ethereal—almost vanishing into the creamy white wall. It seems as weightless as Nancy Corzine's Lucite tables.

FOLLOWING SPREAD: The ceiling in the living room is nine feet and four inches tall, but it looks even taller because I hung the curtains as high as they could go. The vertical Greek-key trim on the leading edge also accentuates their height. I designed the library table for Hickory Chair and placed it by the window, where it can double as a desk. That gives me yet another reason to come into this room. The coffee table is modeled after a design by Jean-Michel Frank and covered in parchment. It's part of the no-color color scheme, which is continued in the white linen on the antique Swedish chairs. All those whites set off the turquoise blue on a nineteenth-century French chair and in the Agra rug from Beauvais Carpets.

ABOVE: At the end of an axis, you need a focal point, and here it's provided by an antique Italian chair. It's the first thing you see as you walk into the living room. OPPOSITE: Then your eye is caught by the fireplace, made by Chesney's in London and modeled after an 1824 drawing in the archives at the Sir John Soane's Museum. The Art Deco andirons add another set of rectangles. I found the Picasso lithograph, printed on corrugated cardboard, at a gallery in Montmartre.

FOLLOWING PAGES: As I put my compositions together, I think about color and shape. LEFT: I was attracted to those little metallic paintings, and I like how they echo the colors in the big painting. That iron sculpture brings it all into balance. RIGHT: A chic French chair brings in a dash of turquoise, and then the urn on top of the French secretary picks up the same color. When I bought that urn years ago from Ainsworth-Noah, I had no idea where I was going to put it. But that particular shade of blue seems to follow me around. And if you love something, it will always find its place.

Frank Zöllner

Leonardo da Vinci

The Complete Paintings and Drawings

TASCHEN

I've always wanted a de Gournay wallpaper and chose a design with flowers and birds for the dining room. The flowers on the fireplace, made in France in the 1800s, echo the same theme. I had it in storage for three years before it found a home here. Amazingly, it was the perfect size for the existing firebox.

OPPOSITE: Both the wallpaper and the fireplace are clearly the work of gifted artisans and show the touch of the hand. The flowers, painted on paper and carved in stone, have a wonderfully whimsical quality. I'm a firm believer in comfortable dining chairs, and these have upholstered backs so you can linger over coffee and conversation. I designed them for Hickory Chair, inspired by a French original. Paintings are casually propped on the mantel, which makes it easy to change the arrangement whenever I feel like it.

FOLLOWING SPREAD: When it comes to tables and chairs, I don't have any qualms about mixing dark wood with light wood. My Choate dining table for Hickory Chair is dark and my Amsterdam chairs are light, but they still work together. They could almost be family pieces, bought at different times, which is far more interesting than a matched set. The 1920s chandelier is by Jansen. To add more sparkle, I designed a ribbon and reed molding, applied to antique mirror, at the cornice line. The ceiling, in a metallic paint by Ralph Lauren, shimmers in candlelight.

ABOVE, CLOCKWISE FROM TOP LEFT: The palette of champagne and platinum blue continues into a bar area off the dining room. These French chairs, made by Jansen in the 1920s and covered in their original leather, were the inspiration for my Amsterdam chairs. An antiqued mirror adds a touch of mystery to a powder room. The tall, slim proportions of the chair, the mirror, and the lamp on the unusual petite French cabinet help elongate the height of the room. OPPOSITE: I found the antique French settee at a Paris flea market and went back to look at it every day before I finally succumbed. It's covered in the same platinum-blue silk canvas as the curtains.

If a piece is chipped, crusty, and crumbling, lead me to it! Age has its advantages when it comes to furniture. There's a kind of patina attained by an object after years of use that can't be duplicated. It has a rough magic that conjures up another place, another time.

OPPOSITE: This Louis XVI limestone mantel comes from the Beaujolais region of France and was made around 1780. It's now installed in my family room, where it brings a kind of weathered strength and maturity into a newly built room. We added this family room, with an adjacent kitchen, onto the back of the house, along with a new master suite above them. These rooms feel more open and expansive, but I was careful not to let them get too big. The scale of the addition is still in proportion to the rest of the house.

FOLLOWING SPREAD: The family room automatically feels relaxed, because there's something so inviting about the two big, comfortable Eugenie sofas, from Verellen. They're slipcovered in Belgian linen, which has such great texture and is practically indestructible. The antique French chair, upholstered in cognac-colored leather, was the start of my flirtation with orange. I picked up the color by adding the Christopher Spitzmiller lamps and an orange tray on the cowhide-covered ottoman. This is a large room so of course you have all this ceiling, and I decided to think of it as an opportunity. We used moldings to create a geometric design. The circle in the center is painted ice blue, and the rest of the squares are that warm champagne color. It puts an interesting lid on the room. The overscaled chandelier is elegant and yet informal, which suits the mood.

ABOVE: Unexpected pairings—like an eighteenth-century tapestry and an antique horn console—can make you see each object with fresh eyes. The pastoral scene turns out to be as fanciful as the table, supported on sculptural intertwining horns. The chairs, too, suddenly read like sculpture in their own way. OPPOSITE: The arrangement of prints and drawings on a wall or vintage globes on an old French drafting table may look haphazard at first, but there's a rhythm to the juxtaposition of large and small, high and low, and there's a balance to the overall shape.

I'm instinctively drawn to certain colors. When it was time to finish the kitchen, I knew I wanted lavender for the linen slipcovers. Just that one burst of color … and it changes with the light. Sometimes it looks more lavender and sometimes it looks more plum. It also has an undertone of gray, which gives a color more depth.

In a kitchen with lots of cool-white marble and bright-white tile, you need something a little softer, like this hand-painted French credenza, to warm it up. The wide walnut plank floors also help, along with old-fashioned details like that little lip on the island's marble top. It reminds me of something you'd see in a Parisian pastry shop. The painting is by Steven Seinberg.

ABOVE: Glass-fronted cabinets add charm. I've always wanted a CornuFé range because they're so beautifully made, almost like a piece of jewelry trimmed in chrome and brass. OPPOSITE: Sun pours into the breakfast area from steel casement windows that look like those you might see in one of those chic, renovated farmhouses in the south of France. Pewter lights hang over an antique Swedish table and reiterate the industrial look.

The library is an interior room with no windows, but we turned that into an advantage by making it quiet and cozy. It's paneled in quartersawn oak and is the place where we go to read and watch TV. Low-slung white leather chairs by Nancy Corzine flank a coffee table made from a vintage Louis Vuitton trunk.

I may have the definitive collection of Eiffel Towers by now. The whole thing started on a whim and I'll admit that they have no particular value to anyone but me. But who could resist? They have such a great shape and it's fascinating to see all the variations people have come up with.

On the upstairs landing, Eiffel Towers are arranged on a round table that is also piled with books. It creates a focal point in a space that you would otherwise just pass through and gives you a reason to stop and take a closer look.

The upstairs sitting room is done in soothing shades of gray and taupe. It's a calm room, a place to reflect or to catch up on work at the vintage campaign desk.

Every bedroom should have a place to sit other than the bed. Even in a small room where there isn't enough space for a chair, you can usually squeeze in a bench at the foot of the bed. I'm lucky. In our bedroom, I could do several seating areas. This one is made for two. It's intimate and inviting, a place where we can have coffee together on a Sunday morning or a glass of wine in the evening while getting dressed for a party.

OPPOSITE: White, silver, and gold—those are the predominant colors in this vignette. And then it's all about shape. That table by Bunny Williams has an interesting hourglass base and the octagonal top is big enough to hold an equally sculptural lamp. The Blossom mirror, by Thomas Pheasant for Baker, looks like a mid-century modern take on a traditional convex mirror. It would make a great piece of jewelry—it sparkles. The Rose Tarlow chairs are upholstered in white silk.

FOLLOWING PAGES, LEFT: I was looking through a file of architectural maps and drawings in an antiques shop in France when I spotted that Braque poster with a gold-leafed dove against a background of blue gray. It became my starting point in the master bedroom, and I took that same blue and used it for the silk curtains and the bed linens and the bed, by Nancy Corzine, trimmed in gold leaf. The bench and the pillow are covered in Fortuny's Delfino. RIGHT: The X detail on the little table is echoed in the X detail above and below the window, where each panel is mirrored to catch the light.

A collection of intaglios, framed in gold and stacked in a grid, proves the power of repetition. They function almost like an architectural element and create a focal point in the hallway that leads to the master bath.

The finish on these elaborately carved antique Russian benches has the crusty look that I love. They became the model for my Anastasia bench for Hickory Chair. I like Fortuny fabric because it has that same handmade quality, and I used it to upholster the seats. The blue silk walls, in the same fabric as the curtains, are a luxurious surprise.

OPPOSITE: I used my Asheworth campaign desk for Hickory Chair as a dressing table in the master bath, topping it with a three-part vanity mirror from Nancy Corzine and a vintage octagonal mirror. Don't miss the dressmaker detail on the curtains, which are laced at the top like an old-fashioned corset. The Alexandra chair, from my collection for Hickory Chair, was named after my daughter. ABOVE, CLOCKWISE FROM TOP LEFT: I went to the couture fashion shows in Paris one year, and the invitations were so imaginative that I framed them. Every surface is an opportunity for another composition. Jewelry is tumbled onto a tray. Mirrors on doors and drawers bring more light into the walk-in closet.

A freestanding tub from the Empire collection by Waterworks has an old-fashioned heft and looks almost like a piece of sculpture under that signature window. Vintage Bagues sconces add a glamorous note. The tables, in bronze doré, used to belong to the Hôtel Georges-V in Paris.

ABOVE: I love pink. It's refreshing, like a strawberry ice cream cone on a hot summer day. Over the years, I had collected various pink things and decided to put them all together in this guest room. A sunny corner offers a place for a friend to read, curled up on my Virginia chair and ottoman for Hickory Chair. A vintage sunburst mirror adds a flash of gold. I designed the Ingrid rug for Safavieh. OPPOSITE: The picture of birds and floating feathers by French artist Paule Marrot was originally a design for a textile. It has been reproduced by Natural Curiosities—a great source for affordable art. I hung it above my Blackland cabinet for Hickory Chair, which hides the TV. The shell-pink curtains, made out of a Nancy Corzine linen, are finished with a crisp white trim.

I like the way French designers will take one fabric and use it everywhere, as I did in this guest room. The fabric, brimming with sunflowers, is by Brunschwig & Fils. My Candler twin bed, designed for Hickory Chair, has an exceptionally tall, upholstered headboard, which looks very French and is also very comfortable. My mirrored Belvedere chest adds a touch of glamour and catches the light. The artwork depicts antique ribbons and is part of my collection for Soicher Marin.

The loggia functions as an outdoor living room, perfect for entertaining. One of our smartest decisions was to build a fireplace and design the seating area around it. We can light a fire on a cool night and linger there for hours.

RIGHT: I wanted a clean, tailored look out here. The Amalfi Tuxedo sofas by Janus et Cie have comfortably deep seats and a vaguely Greco-Roman air. Their strong, graphic lines blend well with the 1950s French woven chairs. I had the dining table custom-made with a weather-resistant zinc top and found vintage chairs to go with it.

FOLLOWING SPREAD: Hydrangeas border the lawn surrounding the pool. I spotted those whimsical wrought-iron chairs at an outdoor flea market in Avignon and bought them on the spot. Now all I have to do is find time to sit there. The garage was designed with French doors and a stone floor to double as a party space. There are guest quarters and a kitchen upstairs.

GLAMOUR

he stately proportions, Venetian plaster walls, and marble floors might lead you to think you're in a villa on Lake Como, but those two-story-tall windows in the living room actually overlook Lake Oliver in Columbus, Georgia. The view is glorious, and the house, designed by Pak Heydt & Associates with a European sensibility, is the very definition of glamour and elegance. But anything done on such a monumental scale can be a little intimidating. The challenge here was to take this very formal house and turn it into a warm, comfortable home for a family with four young children.

I stood in the living room and felt a thrill of excitement because the space was so grand and I knew exactly how to make that work for us. We started from the ground up, with the floors. The marble in the living room and dining room and all through the house was beautiful but rather cold, so we replaced it with kinder, gentler wood—except in the entrance hall. That room, with its soaring ceiling and magnificent double staircase, was truly palatial and we kept it spare, without a lot of furnishings, so you could appreciate the architecture. We wanted you to walk in and feel the extraordinary scale and majesty of the house.

Evoking Italy in all its glory, a Palladian portico frames the front door and creates a grand entrance to this house. The columns, topped by a classical pediment, could feel heavy, but their weight is countered by the way you can see right through the front door to the windows overlooking the lake. That openness makes an imposing home feel light and airy.

Then, in the living room, you're reminded that this is a home. Big, generous sofas and chairs upholstered in tea-colored silk and blue-gray linen velvet are grouped into two seating areas that anchor the large, double-height space. All the walls and the ceiling are done in champagne-colored Venetian plaster to create texture and warmth. Architects Rick Spitzmiller and Robert Norris added more detail to the cornice moldings and designed decorative pediments to crown the doors. In the most elegant way, those details added weight to an exceptionally lofty room and kept it from floating off into the ether.

Luxurious fabrics, luscious colors, old and new furnishings, interesting architectural details—these were the elements we used to build each room. In a house like this, with such generous spaces, the temptation is to fill it up. But I decided to look at it as an artist looks at his canvas, placing each piece of furniture carefully, where it's needed, but leaving plenty of breathing room. More layers may be added naturally, over time, as the family settles into the house, because it's clear that all of these rooms are going to be used. With four children around, you can be sure that many meals will be made in that kitchen and eaten at the French provincial table in the family room.

But the best moment for me was when I saw the four-year-old come zooming through the entrance hall on his scooter—apparently a marble floor makes a very good racetrack. I finally knew we had succeeded in our mission. Clearly, everyone feels comfortable here.

In the entrance hall, the plaster walls are scored to look like stone and a decorative compass is inset into the marble floor. The architecture is so splendid that I decided to defer to it, and furnished the room simply with a pair of custom John Saladino curved benches, one on each side of the doorway to the living room. The bench looks as if it could be carved out of stone but it's actually upholstered in stone-colored silk velvet on the seat—and linen on the legs. The bone-white walls give way to color on the ceiling, which we painted in subtle shades of lavender and blue to give you a surprise when you look up.

Champagne, blue-gray, and a touch of raspberry—those are the kind of colors I see when I'm in Europe. They're muted, faded—more of a feeling than an actual color—and subtle enough that you never get tired of them. They're classic, not trendy.

OPPOSITE: I wanted one rug, rather than two or three, to unify the space so we had a custom carpet made by Beauvais in a champagne color, with a subtle pattern woven through it in blue and gray. It has the same creamy tones as the Venetian plaster on the walls and ceiling, and together they create a quiet envelope. The center table is Italian, circa 1850, and it was the first piece we found for the house. I was delighted to find that Italian gilt-wood mirror, circa 1750, because it has a lot of presence and I needed something strong to hold that wall. A Lucite coffee table adds a contemporary note. The Annecy chandelier is by David Iatesta.

FOLLOWING SPREAD: Those three magnificent windows, with French doors opening to a terrace overlooking the lake, create more than enough drama in the room. That's another reason why I went for subtle colors in the furnishings. The idea was not to overdecorate. You don't want to compete with that view. The curtains are simple—a long fall of blue-gray silk that softens the windows' strong lines. All three sofas—Nancy Corzine's Atherton sofas on the left and John Saladino's Santa Barbara sofa on the right—have the right scale for this large room.

ABOVE: The peonies on the center table add a raspberry accent to the room.
OPPOSITE: Raspberry reappears in the Fortuny fabric on a pair of antique chairs by the fireplace.
The fireplace, designed by Spitzmiller & Norris and carved out of limestone, has a traditional
shape, but the lines are so clean that it looks almost modern. They also added that acanthus frieze
to the cornice. Delicate rock-crystal sconces from Therien & Co. flank a painting by Ivan Olinsky.

This room underwent a radical transformation. When our clients bought the house, it was being used as a media room and was quite dark. We opened it up by installing French doors to the garden. We also added all the moldings and other architectural details. At first I was just planning to do the trim in a metallic paint by Ralph Lauren, but then I liked it so much that I decided to use it on the walls and the ceiling as well. It's the color of the inside of an oyster shell, and it gives the whole room a sheen. The English sideboard, French mirror, and Louis XVI–style chandelier are reflected in the mirrored doors.

An octagonal hallway connecting the family room and the kitchen became a casual breakfast room, with the addition of a marble-topped table and four chairs.

PREVIOUS SPREAD: When we found that Oriental rug for the library, we debated whether to pick up the reds in it or the blues. That deep Prussian blue won out, and now you see it on the club chairs by Dessin Fournir, the throw pillows, and the Christopher Spitzmiller lamp. Our client liked the masculine heft of the Kensington sofas by Restoration Hardware, modeled after a classic Chesterfield. And the leather will only get better with age. Two leather-topped benches by Nancy Corzine double as side tables. Brass library lights from Nessen illuminate the bookshelves and create a warm glow at night.

OPPOSITE: The formality of an antique chest and mirror is counterbalanced by the informality of a sisal rug and slipcovered Bungalow Classic chairs. The mixed message makes the room more intriguing. An aged-iron Sheraton chandelier from Lord & Lockridge stands out as a strong dark note against creamy white walls.

Christopher Peacock designed the kitchen and the pantries. ABOVE, LEFT: The shelves in this pantry can hold plenty of canned goods, so you can see exactly what you have at a glance. Old-fashioned walnut cabinetry hides a refrigerator on the left and more storage on the right. The industrial pendant is from Circa Lighting. ABOVE, RIGHT: The butler's pantry, just off the dining room, is more dressy. The cabinetry is made of limed oak with P. E. Guerin knobs in the center of the doors. OPPOSITE: Looking through a pass-through between the family room and the kitchen, you see the large marble-topped island. A pot rack from Ann-Morris Antiques is within easy reach of the range. We found that antique carved wooden panel and designed the moldings above the stove to frame it.

FOLLOWING PAGES: The patina that's part of certain fabrics and furnishings gives a new house more character. LEFT: The warm tones in the Aubusson tapestry, which dates back to 1750, blend right in with the wood on an antique chest. RIGHT: Hemp curtains—in Michael S. Smith's Indian Flower for Jasper—already have a soft, faded look. We added the coffered ceiling, made of pecky cypress, and the plank floors. The chairs at the French provincial table are slipcovered in linen that ties neatly at the sides, like an elegant bib.

A great piece of furniture, like this chinoiserie desk, can carry a room. It adds style, sophistication, and a touch of the exotic.

OPPOSITE: I found the desk at Mrs. Howard in Atlanta and paired it with a Canzone side chair from Dennis & Leen. They don't really match, but they both have character and that makes the combination work.

FOLLOWING SPREAD: The study is paneled in limed oak, and I decided to paint the ceiling turquoise, which is not a typical choice. But I thought the ceiling needed something to distinguish it, since the paneling is so strong. The linen curtains with turquoise trim pick up the same shades. The room is traditional, with old standbys like a tufted leather chair and ottoman, but it's not stuffy. The Park Avenue sofa and Lakewood lounge chairs are from the Cameron Collection, and the Paris wing chair is by Scalamandré. The custom mantel is carved with birds.

PREVIOUS PAGES: Accessories help tell the story. LEFT: A collection of tortoiseshell boxes says that a person with an eye for beauty—and unexpected combinations—lives here. Who would think that a chinoiserie desk and a tortoiseshell box would have so much in common? RIGHT: The antique wood finials have a nicely battered look and add a sense of age to the room. I like the idea of graphic pillows, juxtaposed with traditional furniture. They bring a contemporary edge to the ensemble.

RIGHT: The master bedroom is done in what might be the most unusual colors I've ever worked with. It started with that Fortuny fabric that now hangs behind the bed. It's in the most beautiful shades of lavender and gray. Then I found that incredible dark gray-lavender silk—Grappa from Great Plains—for the curtains, and finished it off with a band of brighter lavender. An antique headboard was gilded and upholstered in the same silk.

ABOVE: Some people might think that the Pluie chandelier, from Allan Knight, is a little over-the-top for a closet. Not me. It's so much fun! We covered my Alexandra chair for Hickory Chair in lavender silk, to pick up on the lavender in the master bedroom. OPPOSITE: The Doric columns from the exterior of the house make another appearance in the master bath, where they frame the tub. Luxuriously encased in marble, the tub comes with a great view. The beautifully arched steel-framed window was made by Crittall, an English company founded in 1849. There's something very satisfying about the traditional locking mechanism they use. It makes me feel as if I'm in Europe.

AUTHENTIC

Stone floors, white plank walls, and beams the size of tree trunks—the entrance hall in this Atlanta house by architect William T. Baker makes a striking first impression. It feels a bit like one of those great Arts and Crafts houses designed by Edwin Lutyens or C.F.A. Voysey in England around the turn of the last century. But the ceilings here are even taller and the proportions of the rooms even more loft-like—it's a modern take on a wonderfully old-world, handcrafted style.

When I walked in, I responded to the strength and simplicity of the materials and thought the furnishings should have the same kind of character. I wanted to find pieces that had their own sculptural quality. That way they wouldn't get lost in the tall, airy rooms. A high-backed Jacobean chair in the living room embodies a certain elegance of proportion. A trestle table in the entrance hall looks a little rough, but it's just as elegant because of its simple, functional shape. You can feel the uneven surface of the wood, and everywhere you look there are interesting textures—the natural linen on the chairs, the old gilt on a mirror, the iron frame of a coffee table. It all contributes to the feeling of authenticity I wanted to create in these rooms.

In this view from the living room, looking through the entrance hall to the front door, you can see the power of the architecture. Raw cypress timbers frame the doorway. I decided to keep the decoration similarly spare. The deer antlers have a natural grace and beauty and look almost like a piece of sculpture. Curves are juxtaposed with straight lines. Both are combined in the silhouette of the Jacobean-style Barbini armchairs from Holland & Co.

The architecture may have echoes of the Arts and Crafts era, but it also evokes simple utilitarian structures like stables and barns. This house is not confined to any one style or period, and neither are the interiors. Instead, I like to play up the differences between one object and another, creating all sorts of juxtapositions of rough and smooth, dark and light, rustic and refined. The contrasts are unexpected, and they create a kind of energy. It's surprising to see a crystal chandelier in a room that appears to be paneled with barn siding. Moments like that give me a little shiver of excitement. They make the space come alive.

ABOVE: In the arched door and casement windows of the house, you can spot overtones of English Arts and Crafts. OPPOSITE: The entrance hall, with its raw-wood ceiling and tumbled-limestone floor, feels like a transitional space—half-indoors and half-outdoors. The monochromatic palette and natural textures are a nod to Belgian style. Flanking the cypress-framed doorway to the living room is a pair of carved and gilded Baroque overdoors, made in Austria circa 1700, that epitomize the contrast of the rustic and the refined. I found those at Lief in Los Angeles.

Light and dark, rough and smooth, gilded or matte—the one constant holding everything together in this composition is that each piece has an interesting shape. Even the lampshade is unusually elongated.

I like the way the arms of the Charlotte chair by Verellen swoop up and out—taking the familiar silhouette of a wing chair and playing with it a bit. Suddenly, it feels more contemporary. The Bastille console from Formations is based on an antique trestle table and yet it, too, feels almost modern in its shape. Its straight, simple lines contrast with the elaborate, gilded curlicues of the Austrian overdoor.

As you step from the entrance hall into
the large, double-height living room, it's a
dramatic moment. In order to make
the room feel even taller, we whitewashed
the wood on the ceiling. If left natural, it
would have put a lid on the room. This way,
the beams almost disappear, creating a
white-architectural envelope that lets you
see the space as a whole. The room is
overscaled, as are the furnishings and the
stone fireplaces at each end. Nancy Corzine's
Atherton sofas are big and comfortable, piled
with pillows. The antiqued mirrors, almost
as tall as the windows, are topped with a
graphic motif that feels half-modern and
half–Chinese Chippendale.

Where are we? Is this a dining room or a barn? There's a delightful ambiguity to this room, where the walls are covered in wood siding that looks as if it could be part of a horse stall, and yet they're hung with fine art and lit by a crystal chandelier.

PREVIOUS SPREAD: The hand-blocked print on the curtains, Tashkent by Robert Kime, is also overscaled. Made with vegetable dyes, it already looks nicely faded. It gave me the color direction for the room. I picked up the blue on a wing chair, in the Fortuny throw pillows, and in the striped cushions on a pair of 1950s Scandinavian leather campaign chairs from Lief. I didn't want the room to feel too formal. The chairs can move between the two seating areas, depending on where they're needed. But I chose one large rug, one chandelier, and treated the three French doors as one window, to unify the space. A high-backed Tuscan sofa by John Saladino, next to the fireplace on the left, is another of those pieces that blurs the line between antique and modern. It reminds me of the classic Knole sofa, reimagined in a more rectilinear, contemporary way. The paintings over both mantels are by Raphaëlle Goethals.

OPPOSITE: The disconnect between the art and the walls creates a kind of tension that makes the room intriguing. The wood is not as rough as it could be—the limed finish gives it a creamy tone. The Fontaine chandelier is from Dennis & Leen. The painting is by Thrush Holmes.

Something fascinating happens when you layer all these beautifully sophisticated things in a room paneled like a barn. Pale tea-colored silk curtains are lined in the same linen that covers the Gustavian-style dining chairs, circa 1890. The chairs pick up the color of the footed stone base of the Michael Taylor table. I like the stone because it seems to reiterate the strength of the walls. The silhouette of the black limestone fireplace stands out against the limed wood. At first glance, Colonial-style iron sconces don't seem to go with a gilded sunburst mirror, but again, the contrast is what interests me. I like the plain lines of the antique secretary. It offers lots of storage and can double as a buffet. The rug covering the ebonized wood floor is an Egyptian Sultanabad from Moattar.

Somehow the kitchen manages to look both antique and modern. The painted plank walls and the style of the cabinetry feels old-fashioned, but then the sharp graphic X at the end of the island strikes a more contemporary note. Cone-shaped bronze pendants and a stainless-steel hood look industrial, but then I added a pair of lamps that feel more cozy and create a sense of intimacy. The ebonized wood floor continues in from the adjacent dining room and makes the whites look even whiter. Barstools are slipcovered in tobacco-colored linen to pick up on that dark note.

ABOVE: A breakfast table, topped with dark gray limestone, separates the kitchen from the family room. I slipcovered my Chastain chairs for Hickory Chair in a striped linen that has the look and feel of a dishcloth. OPPOSITE: Held together by structural steel cables, the ceiling in the family room soars. Shades of ivory, taupe, brown, and black make up the palette. There's just a hint of blue in the curtain fabric, Montague by Rose Tarlow, but again it has that faded look. Flax-colored linen covers the sofa and the chairs. Flax becomes the background color and keeps the large room looking light and airy.

I like to use dressmaker details to add a little charm and make a room feel special. The linen slipcover on the settee ties over the legs like a ballerina's toe shoes.

The master bedroom is all about the play of subtle colors and alluring textures. I chose platinum silk from J. Robert Scott for the curtains, and the silk carpet from Mansour picks up the same tone, with a hint of lavender. Polished nickel, brass, and mirror on my Austell floor lamp and a vintage coffee table add a little sparkle. The throw, made of Mongolian lamb's wool, adds an exotic touch.

RIGHT: In a large room with a great wooden roof like a barn, I decided to do a few large pieces. The Belaire French settee has long, graceful lines and a lovely undulating curve to the seat. I had the headboard custom-made with curved sides, like a wing chair, and upholstered it in platinum velvet from J. Robert Scott in the same color as the silk curtains. The bed linens were custom-made by Leontine Linens. Pillows pick up the lavender, used as an accent. The Percival chandelier in rusted iron and whitewashed wood, from my collection for Visual Comfort, was modeled after a French original.

FOLLOWING PAGES: The pale, ephemeral palette carries through to the master bathroom. LEFT: An unusual window above the vanity is a natural source of overhead light. To make the rest of the wall feel as luminous, we covered it in antiqued mirror. Then I hung an antique Venetian mirror, shaped like a faceted jewel, on top. RIGHT: An arched alcove adds a touch of fantasy and frames a freestanding tub. The silver and lavender in the curtains echo the antiqued mirror and the lavender walls.

124

ABOVE: The daughter wanted a black-and-white bedroom and loved this Bradley Hughes fabric, which looks completely traditional until you notice the skulls. And then we added hot pink, for a little jolt. A dressing table from Brocade Home doubles as a desk. OPPOSITE: A whimsical arched alcove is big enough to accommodate an extra bed for sleepovers. It's also the perfect place to curl up and read.

OPPOSITE: In the old days, you'd wash up by pouring water from a pitcher into a bowl. The washstand in the guest bathroom is fitted with two vessel sinks to create the same feeling. It's an interesting contrast to the sleek glass shower stall. Plain linen curtains are trimmed with raffia and wooden beads. ABOVE: Sliding barn doors give the guest bedroom a warm, rustic look. I chose the bed linens for that charming appliqué that reminds me of a 1940s bedspread.

When both sets of doors are open, the pool house feels more like a pavilion. An outdoor fireplace takes the chill off the evening air and draws people to the comfortable seating area.

ABOVE: The overscaled pattern on Katie Ridder's Leaf wallpaper makes the small pool house bathroom feel much larger. Exotic lanterns and a vessel sink add to the bohemian atmosphere.
OPPOSITE: In the pool house kitchen, the rustic mood takes on a contemporary edge. The canvas light fixture from Bungalow may be hung a bit primitively on rope but it has a modern, elongated shape. I like its scale and the way it looks against the window grid. The wrought-iron sconces are elongated as well, which makes them look more modern. That distinctive handle on the back of the barstools, designed by Bobby McAlpine, makes them easy to move.

CHIC

Deep, rich, saturated color—that's what makes this house memorable. And the colors we chose—turquoise, lavender, purple, orange—are chic and sophisticated. They make a new house in Greenwich, Connecticut, look more like something you'd see on the Left Bank in Paris. Actually, this house, designed by architect Joan Chan for a young couple with three children, feels very French. It has tall proportions, elegant moldings that look very eighteenth-century, and classical limestone chimneypieces. But it also has something else, something more intangible. It has style.

A lot of that style comes from color. Paint is one of the most powerful tools we possess and yet few people are brave enough to take advantage of it. When I first met these clients, the wife showed me a picture she had saved of a dining room I had done where the walls were painted a deep, rich turquoise. When you walked into that room, you were immersed in color. As soon as I saw that picture, I was thrilled because that meant this client was willing to do something out of the ordinary. She was willing to be bold.

But that doesn't mean you have to be bold everywhere. In this house, we used color strategically. There are moments of excitement, but then you have to balance them with moments of calm. In the living room, the envelope is neutral. The walls

Looking from the living room into the dining room, you get an intense shot of color. A gilded marble-topped table made in France in 1880 gives the room a sense of history. With a pair of neoclassical-style benches beside it, the table becomes more than a surface for display. You could actually sit here and look through one of the art books. Or the benches can be moved where needed, to provide extra seating.

are painted the color of an elephant's tusk. The furniture is upholstered in shades of champagne and ivory and the custom rug picks up the same tones. Only a few throw pillows and the paintings flanking the fireplace give you a hint of the colors to come.

As you walk through the house, the rooms segue from saturated colors to paler tones. Sometimes the color will be on the walls. At other times it will be on the upholstery. The variations create a rhythm and a flow. Colors appear and then reappear, in a slightly different shade. And something interesting happens. You come away with the impression that there is a lot more color in this house than there actually is. If you were to analyze each room, you'd realize that the background colors are usually neutral. But that's not what the eye recalls. The eye goes straight to the blues and the purples and the oranges, which create the drama.

The furnishings are meant to catch your attention as well. Pieces like an Empire-style settee and a neoclassical Madame Récamier–style chaise suggest other times and places. A bench upholstered in three blocks of color—lavender, cream, and lavender—has a French flair. The rooms are my usual mix of antique and modern, because that's the way we live today. Some pieces we buy new. Others we inherit. And others have been collected over the years. I don't know many people who limit themselves to one era and want to live in a pure eighteenth-century or early-American room. Life—and decorating—is more exciting when there are no limits.

OPPOSITE: In the dining room, everything—including the built-in cabinetry—is painted a fabulous shade of turquoise and lacquered to give it even more depth. The dining chairs are trimmed in the same color. I like the idea of putting an almost gaudy carved and gilded frame on a Picasso lithograph casually done on corrugated cardboard.

FOLLOWING SPREAD: Finding a turquoise silk for the gilded loveseat that would match the walls was a challenge. David Iatesta's Venetian chandelier hangs in front of a Louis XV limestone chimneypiece. My Choate dining table for Hickory Chair was inspired by a Regency piece and is done in walnut with gilded edges. The ink drawing is by Franz Kline.

Why is that little sofa in a corner?
Because I like to create different places
to sit in a room. You feel the space in
a whole different way when you're
looking at it from this intimate nook.

OPPOSITE: The furniture, including my Leigh sofa for Hickory Chair, is all covered in shades of ivory that blend right into the walls. Only the turquoise linen velvet throw pillows give you a preview of the saturated color to come in the adjacent dining room. The curtains, in Holland & Sherry's duchesse silk, are trimmed with the same Greek-key motif that borders the Chinese Peony carpet from Beauvais. I like that painting by Nancy Lorenz because it has the same ethereal quality as the room. It's made with gold leaf, mother-of-pearl, and pigment and relates to the gilded antiques, but in a contemporary way.

FOLLOWING SPREAD: The Louis XVI chimneypiece adds detail and texture to a new living room and makes it feel older and more European. Two sofas by John Saladino are slipcovered in champagne-colored silk. The blue, purple, pink, and orange that you see in the paintings by Aaron Wexler will reappear in other rooms. Nancy Corzine's Balthazar chandelier adds a glimmer of silver.

144

Purple is the accent that makes the ivory tones look even paler. In a room with very little pattern, I decided to drape the consoles on each side of the fireplace with fabric. It's a contemporary version of an old-world damask and adds a lush note alongside the neoclassical recamier.

OPPOSITE: The antique recamier has such elegant lines, almost like a piece of sculpture. It suggests another era and gives that corner of the room a little history. The purple Manuel Canovas silk on the pillow seems to come straight out of the painting and makes the recamier look almost contemporary. And then I went back in time with the lavender fabric that drapes the console. It was designed by Sabina Fay Braxton to look like an antique textile.

FOLLOWING PAGES, LEFT: The hints of purple we've already seen in the living room culminate in this intimate seating area next to the bar. I upholstered the wall in the same purple silk I used on the pillows and designed a high-backed banquette to fit the niche, upholstering it in a deep, rich aubergine mohair. With an antique sunburst mirror and little swing-arm sconces, the seating area looks like a sophisticated supper club in Paris. RIGHT: The bar is upholstered in creamy leather and topped in onyx. An antiqued mirror on the wall adds more atmosphere and reflects two 1960s metal sculptures that are kind of weird—and wonderful.

The books on the table read "LOUIS VUITTON: MARC JACOBS" and "LUXURY STORES: TOP IN THE WORLD"

Leather-bound books and tiger maple paneling create a sense of tradition in the library—and then I added a little blue velvet. It makes a room that could have been very formal feel rather dashing.

OPPOSITE: Instead of the typical dull brown desk, I chose this elegant piece in ebonized walnut and brass—L'Architecte desk by Baker—based on a 1950s original by French designer André Arbus. The floating top can tilt up like a drafting table. Beside it, two of my Hunt chairs for Hickory Chair are upholstered in a Holland & Sherry cotton velvet. Nailheads accentuate their curves. The curtains, in a Holland & Sherry wool, are trimmed with caramel tape across the top and along the leading edge to pick up the color of the paneling. The large wooden ball on the floor is just something I found. It's that unexpected object that makes the room feel chic.

FOLLOWING PAGES, LEFT: Color adds interest to a long hallway. The lavender silk at the window, from my fabric collection for Lee Jofa, is also used to upholster an antique bench. It's done in blocks of color, with my oyster silk in the middle, to make it feel more contemporary. The walls are hung with a series of Cy Twombly prints. RIGHT: In the powder room, vintage Bagues sconces pick up the gleam of the Gracie wallpaper, hand-painted on the most beautiful shade of lavender. The vanity is made from a slab of onyx, with a river of color running through it in the same gold as the fixtures, mixed with lavender and blue-gray.

A contemporary work of art by
Ellsworth Kelly is casually propped on
an antique French mantel. The vivid
blocks of color make a bold statement.
Art animates the room.

The only serious antiques in the family room are the chimneypiece and the French chandelier, but they're
enough to give the room a traditional context. The walls are painted a beautiful bone color that
matches the limestone. Then I livened things up with bright pillows and furnishings that occupy that
interesting space between antique and modern, like that high-backed wing chair. Made by Dennis & Leen,
it's based on a traditional English shape, but it looks more contemporary in pale blue Edelman leather.

YVES SAINT LAURENT

AMERICAN FASHION

PHOTOGRAPHS

Orange seems to dominate the family room, but when you analyze it, the orange is only in four pillows and a Hermès blanket. Everything else is neutral. The George V sofas by Holly Hunt and the Michael chairs from Bungalow Classic are covered in natural linen. It's a tall room, and I decided to break up the length of the curtains with two colors. The block of blue-gray linen at the bottom anchors the room and creates a virtual wainscoting.

OPPOSITE: With a concrete top and a mirrored back, the Saltire console by Bobby McAlpine is a contemporary version of a traditional console. I topped it with a horn lamp because I liked the sinuous curves against the table's right angles. It also plays off the colors and shapes in the Cy Twombly lithograph. ABOVE: Ralph Lauren designed these modern interpretations of an old hurricane lantern in more sumptuous materials—brass, leather, and bronze.

Cantilevered shelves are great for displaying a constantly changing array of artwork in the children's study. A bulletin board covered in colorful fabric instead of plain cork also makes it easy to pin things up.

OPPOSITE: Right off the family room is a smaller space, dedicated to the children's activities. It's a good place for doing homework uninterrupted, sitting on my Amsterdam chairs for Hickory Chair at the built-in desk. Lemon-yellow walls pick up the yellow in the fabrics and make it feel cheerful. And when a school project is in full swing, you can shut the mirrored French doors to close off any mess.

FOLLOWING SPREAD: The kitchen is spacious, with a beautiful stone floor and a huge stone chimneypiece over the range. Details like the turned legs at the corners of the island, the country French iron hardware, and the hand-forged iron lanterns from Gregorius Pineo give it an old-fashioned look. My Amsterdam counter stools are covered in faux leather, which wipes clean easily.

The Branch chandelier, by
Paul Ferrante, adds a fanciful
note to the breakfast room. It
looks very light, in contrast to
the dining table, which looks
very heavy. The table, from
Restoration Hardware, was
modeled after a seventeenth-
century original found in
a monastery. You can do
practically anything to the
top and it will still look great.
The antique chairs have
beautifully curved caned
backs. The same blue-gray
linen that was on the curtains
in the family room reappears
here. I hung pewter chargers
on the walls, since there was
no room for art.

OPPOSITE: That stone chimneypiece in the corner of the kitchen may look antique, but it actually houses the latest must-have accessory—a pizza oven. The Charlotte chairs from Bungalow Classic are slipcovered in natural linen. ABOVE: The lamp picks up a color in the small Carolyn Carr painting, displayed on an easel in front of the window.

169

The sitting area in the master bedroom is a composition in soft, solid colors like ice blue and sterling. All of the pattern is in the accessories—a chandelier made out of circles, a mirror rimmed in silvery wooden spokes, graphic throw pillows, a verre églomisé coffee table, and an ottoman trimmed with an Art Deco motif. The carpet is by Stark.

170

Luxurious materials add
to the allure in the master
bedroom. A lacquered
headboard by Nancy
Corzine is upholstered
in sterling-colored silk
from J. Robert Scott. The
duvet and pillows in linen
velvet from Lili Alessandra
pick up the same silvery
shade. Nancy Corzine also
designed the streamlined
version of a traditional
chaise, upholstered in silk
velvet. French doors open
to a balcony overlooking
the garden. The watercolor
is by Carolyn Carr.

OPPOSITE: With that stunning slab of onyx on the wall, we really didn't need much else in the husband's bathroom. The cantilevered vanity is made out of rosewood. I found the 1930s French chair in an antiques shop in Atlanta. It may be a little unexpected, but it works perfectly.
ABOVE: The seat in her bathroom is just as unusual. Designed by Jonathan Adler, it has a Lucite base and is covered in Mongolian lamb's wool. A glass mosaic around the tub, the mirrored walls, and a mirrored vanity add sparkle.

CLASSIC

I f you're thinking about building a house, one of the smartest things you can do is to get an interior designer involved from the very beginning, along with the architect. The two may approach a room from different perspectives, but both want the same result—a great house—and it's an advantage when everyone's ideas are folded in from the start. Then you will be much more likely to wind up with a home that not only looks good but also suits the way you and your family actually live.

It's the way I like to work, and that's how we did this project. The clients were living in Atlanta and planning a move to Greenwich, Connecticut, where they had found a wonderful piece of property and decided to build a new house. But rather than hire people they did not know, they chose to put their team together here in Atlanta. So architects Bill Harrison and Greg Palmer, along with me, were part of this project from the ground up.

The architects designed a very appealing, traditional house—built of clapboard and fieldstone, with beautifully proportioned rooms and lovely details like arched doorways and egg-and-dart moldings. It's an American classic, and I wanted to furnish it in a way that stayed true to that tradition, yet still felt fresh enough for a family with four young children.

I took many of the colors in the living room from this gorgeous fabric—Scalamandré's Meissen, imported from Italy. The flowering branch design was inspired by Meissen porcelain.

The concept is simple. Antiques—like the fabulous Oushak rugs in the living room, the dining room, the family room, and the library—set the tone, and then I pulled out some lively colors like tangerine, aquamarine, and raspberry to add a more youthful note. A pair of sofas in the living room is upholstered in discreet alabaster-colored linen velvet, the kind of thing you would expect to find in an elegant room like this. But then two antique armchairs by the window feel years younger, covered in a raspberry and cream linen velvet.

It all proves my point. Tradition doesn't have to be stuffy. A house can be formal and still feel inviting. The dining room is the perfect illustration. It has all the proper elements—hand-painted wallpaper, antique furniture, a crystal chandelier. And then we added a touch of fantasy with a mirrored Chinese Chippendale wainscot. It's an enchanting detail. It turns a solid wall into light.

All through the house, you'll see a certain restraint, characteristic of old East Coast houses, coupled with charm. None of the rooms feels cluttered or overdone. The traditional setting may be familiar—after all, that's part of its appeal. But there is always something out of the ordinary—a delicate wallpaper, a beautiful fabric, a bright color—to catch the eye. Pretty is one of those words that may sound a little old-fashioned these days, but I like it. And this is an unabashedly pretty house.

A rosewood pedestal table, made in France circa 1810, anchors the entryway. I deliberately left the dark walnut floor bare, to create a strong, simple contrast to the creamy white walls. The Montecito lantern is from Formations.

Subtle colors—like the delicate tint of these roses—work well as a background in a room. Then I will add brighter colors in the fabrics and furnishings as an accent.

OPPOSITE: When it comes to flower arrangements, I like to keep it simple—just one type of flower, in one color. I think it has more impact.

FOLLOWING SPREAD: Blue is the accent color in the living room. You see it on the trumeau hanging over the fireplace, on the Fortuny pillows on the sofas, and on the leading edge of the silk taffeta curtains. The Bernard sofas are by Nancy Corzine. The mirrored top of the coffee table makes it feel light and adds some more sparkle. The Dupont chandelier is from Dennis & Leen.

ABOVE: The butler's pantry is done in a complementary wallpaper that picks
up on the same shade of tangerine used in the adjacent dining room.
OPPOSITE: Hand-painted wallpaper in the dining room has a weathered patina
and looks like something you might see on the walls of a Venetian palazzo. It's the
Aviatrix pattern from Arena Design. Mirrored wainscoting adds a little gleam.

The tangerine in the dining room started with the Oushak rug, circa 1890. Then we custom colored the wallpaper to match and found tangerine silk for the curtains. The client already owned the dining chairs but the wood was too dark for the room. So we had them washed with bone-colored paint and then upholstered them in taupe mohair, with no trim—very pure and simple. There was already enough color in the room. A Louis XV bronze and crystal chandelier hangs over an English Regency table. The arched door is mirrored, to make the room feel larger.

For a decorator like Sister Parish, a traditional room wouldn't be complete without one of her favorite animal prints. I love them, too. The pattern is so strong and it adds a wild note.

I chose a tiger print by Nancy Corzine to cover a chair in the library. The handsome paneling is made of quartersawn oak, limed to accentuate the grain. Antique prints add a nice counterpoint to the books.

Once again, I pulled the color palette for
a room out of an antique Oushak rug. A
navy chenille sofa in the library is flanked
by camel-colored club chairs. The curtains
are made of a Holland & Sherry tweed that
reminded me of a man's suit. Antique pieces,
like the game table and chairs, add a little
history. Of course, the oak paneling and
the coffered ceiling also help. The Duveaux
chandelier is from Dessin Fournir.

ABOVE: The client owned a hand-painted canvas screen that we flattened out and hung on the wall of the family room. I picked up that green in the fabric on the lounge chairs. The soft fawn-colored linen velvet on the sofa takes its color from the antique Oushak rug, found at Moattar. And then I went in a completely different direction for the curtains, choosing the bold, graphic Imperial Trellis, designed by Kelly Wearstler for Schumacher. OPPOSITE: The fireplace has such an interesting shape that everything else around had to live up to it. There's something inherently intriguing about a curved back on a square-seated chair, and that's part of the charm of the George III corner chair. To cover the wing chair, I chose Wallace Vine linen, designed by Michael S. Smith for Jasper, because it reminded me of the pattern on the screen. The mirror reflects a Clinton chandelier by Paul Ferrante. The candlesticks and mirror may be antique, but the forms are so strong and sculptural that they feel almost contemporary.

A trestle table with wing chairs at the head and foot gives the breakfast room an early-American look. The ceiling is a warm goldenrod color, inspired by the Bennison fabric on the curtains. All the folds in the curtain make it hard to appreciate the pattern, which is why I always like to do one piece where you can see the fabric laid out flat, as on that bench. The iron Mansfield chandelier, by David Iatesta, has a primitive quality that makes it feel like a period piece.

The hammered metal
pendants and wooden stools
add a dark, contrasting note
to a creamy white kitchen.
The marble counter on the
island is finished off with an
ogee edge, to give it an old-
fashioned look.

199

If only every house came equipped with such a carefully thought-out mudroom. There are plenty of places where you can sit and pull off your boots, plus a wall of wooden lockers for coats and all sorts of sports equipment. And the floor is slate, which is impervious to dirt.

The way the benches are carved reminds me of church pews. We tucked more storage underneath the seats and a shelf on top can hold bags and hats. The whitewashed lantern is by Paul Ferrante.

Aquamarine is one of the clients' favorite colors and we chose it for the fabrics and painted it on the ceiling of the master bedroom. The Louis XVI headboard by Dennis & Leen is upholstered in aquamarine linen. Embroidered linen curtains are done in the same shade. Pure white bed linens always feel fresh to me. Nancy Corzine's Richelieu bench is covered in Minton by Cowtan & Tout. Antique rose medallion lamps stand on new mirrored chests by Panache.

202

ABOVE: White Thassos marble tile laid in a chevron pattern picks up the palest color in the hand-painted de Gournay wallpaper—the pattern is Badminton—in the master bath. The silk shade over the tub is controlled electronically.
OPPOSITE: Tiny pearl buttons run up the back of a slipper chair. The crystal candlestick lamps flanking the dressing table mirror are from Edgar-Reeves.

ABOVE, LEFT: A daughter's bedroom is decorated in luscious shades of peppermint pink, with a headboard upholstered in a delicate floral and bed hangings in a smart check. ABOVE, RIGHT: The doors in the wife's walk-in closet have monogrammed knobs. I love special details like that. OPPOSITE: A window hung with silk taffeta curtains makes the closet feel more like a room. Polished nickel sconces from Palmer Hargrave and mirrored panels on the cabinetry catch the light.

NATURAL

S and, sea, and sky—that's the view from the windows of this beach house near Charleston, South Carolina. In a simple, sunlit place like this, you feel very close to nature, and it seemed appropriate to use natural materials like wood, wicker, jute, and linen. And I wanted to use colors you see outside because the house is very open to the landscape, with French doors everywhere and wide, wraparound porches. Even when you're in the house it feels almost as if you're out on the water, and it just seemed right that the inside and the outside of the house should relate to each other.

I chose all sorts of blue and white and sand-colored fabrics and comfortable slipcovered furniture. But this is not your typical beach house. It's not cute and it's not casual in that tossed-together, just-for-the-season way. The furniture is a little more serious because this is more than a weekend house. Eventually, the clients plan to live here full-time, and the house was designed by the architect Bill Huey with that in mind. I also kept that thought as we did each room. Some of the furnishings are antique and some are modern, but they're all solid, substantial pieces that will last forever. When you walk through the door, it feels like a warm, welcoming home.

Out on the porch, a teak table is always ready for an impromptu
gathering. The family and their guests can sit back in one of the sturdy
director's chairs and feel the sea breeze.

ABOVE: The house is built on three levels, with the main public rooms on the second floor to take advantage of the view. To get there, you climb a staircase inside a turret, one of the lovely old-fashioned touches—along with white-painted shiplap—that make the house feel as if it has been there forever. OPPOSITE: I'll often put a table in an entry because it's so practical to have a place to set down your keys. The strong, simple contrast of dark floors and white walls is echoed in the colors of the striped jute rug.

Look at all the different textures—the driftwood mirror, the linen curtains, the custom-designed wool striped rug, the rattan chairs, the weathered wood on the antique Belgian buffet and the refectory table. It all feels very plain and elemental. Even the bowls on the table look utterly natural, as if they were carved out of petrified tree trunks.

Instead of a separate, formal living room and dining room, this house has a more open plan, with the living area, dining area, and kitchen in one long rectangular space. At the midpoint, I placed this dining table from Gregorius Pineo. It's more than just a place to eat. It's a place to hang out and play games, catch up on work, or read the paper. That's why I wanted those rattan chairs. They're big and comfortable, so you can sit and stay a while. The driftwood mirror, the lamp, and the buffet help define this area as a room. I put the mirror on a stand so it doesn't get in the way of the curtains. A blue band along the leading edge of the curtains echoes the blue stripe in the rug.

The living area has a casual elegance, with a limestone fireplace and a pair of Verellen sofas slipcovered in rustic linen. A custom rug picks up the colors you'd see if you look out the windows. It's in shades of sand, sea, and sun-bleached driftwood, with a thin line of orange like the sunset. Blue and orange are the accent colors that animate the room.

216

Some of the furniture in the hallway is new and some is old, but all the various pieces come together to create a focal point in what would be just a passageway without them.

A pair of nineteenth-century Italian armchairs, flanking a new console table, makes the upstairs hallway feel more like a room. I like the hand-painted, free-form designs on the Hispano-Moresque pottery from Formations and thought it offered a nice contrast to the more straitlaced 1940s mirror. Blue accents, like those on the antique Oushak rug, run throughout the house.

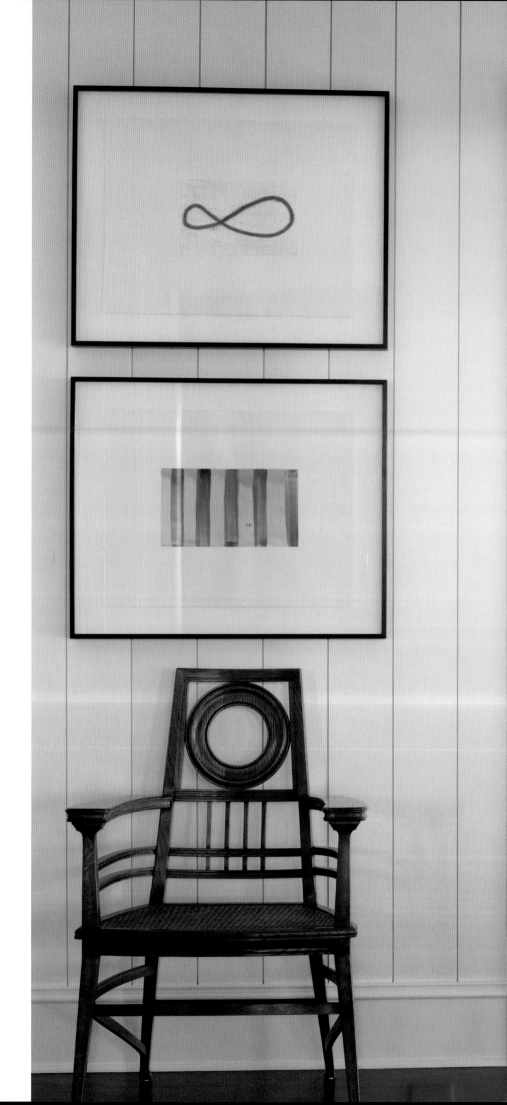

Contemporary painters do not have a
monopoly on abstract geometry. Look at the
circles and squares on Michael S. Smith's
Maya chair. It's like a new version of a
wonderful old Arts and Crafts piece. The
vertical lines of the shiplap suddenly look
abstract as well. The two paintings on the
left are by Don Maynard. The collage on the
right is by Cecil Touchon.

222

ABOVE: Every guest room should open onto a porch like this, with a sofa that swings from the ceiling and lounge chairs with arms big enough to hold a drink, all from Sutherland. I couldn't resist the coffee table, made from bits of driftwood. The combination of striped and solid pillows and the geometric rug pick up the blue and white theme. OPPOSITE: In a guest bedroom, blue paint goes partway up a white wall, like wainscoting. This is a detail I've seen in European country houses. More blue and white fabric covers my Nanette chair and the pillows on the four-poster. A lightweight Moroccan rug takes the place of a duvet.

ABOVE: The master bedroom, another octagonal room with built-in drama, is all pale blues and creams. Rose Tarlow's Beecham chair is covered in a printed linen by Pintura Studio. The curtains are made from a C&C Milano linen with a stripe you can barely see. OPPOSITE: The two posters on Thomas Pheasant's bed for Baker stretch up toward the peaked ceiling. In such an architecturally strong room, you need strong pieces—like the Otley mirror from Dessin Fournir and the Montecito lantern from Formations. I like dark wood against white walls, and the blues and the creams are soothing. You fall asleep to the sound of the sea.

ABOVE: Lots of children, including cousins and friends, can squeeze into the bunk beds. The shelves in the center double as a ladder. The striped rug is by Stark. OPPOSITE: In the family room, red, white, and blue set up a nautical theme. Vintage boat prints and a mirror from Bungalow Classic are hung on nautical rope from a custom iron picture rail. The table in the corner is perfect for puzzles and games.

RELAXED

Blackberry Farm is a very special place. Thirty years ago, Sandy and Kreis Beall bought a small country inn tucked away in the foothills of the Smoky Mountains in Tennessee, and now it's grown into a Relais & Chateaux estate, famed for its cuisine. But they haven't forgotten the simple country pleasures—guests can eat just-laid eggs and homemade sausages for breakfast, then go off horseback riding or fly-fishing or help pick vegetables in the garden or just sit on the porch with a book. The Bealls have a gift for making everyone feel like family.

I've been working with them for ten years, first helping Sandy and Kreis with their own house and various other buildings, and now doing the same for their son Sam and his wife, Mary Celeste, who have taken over the management of the idyllic 4,200-acre farm. Sam and Mary Celeste are constantly inviting guest chefs from all over the country to come teach a cooking class and inevitably everyone winds up over at their house, so it had to be not only a family house (to accommodate their five children) but also ready to entertain multitudes at the drop of a hat. Sam had fond memories of a house he once lived in as a child, which had an unusual layout. Instead of a formal entry, you walked straight into the dining room. Right away, it said that place was all

Next to the fireplace in the living room, these antique English library steps act as a kind of pedestal for a casual arrangement of objects that are special to the owners—a painting, vintage brass candlesticks, old books. The Napoleon III lady's chair, made in France circa 1860, is a little art object in itself and is upholstered in slate-blue strié velvet from Scalamandré.

The idea was to make the house look as if it had been there forever. Fieldstone found on the property adds a rustic note to the facade. Doric columns and tall triple-hung windows suggest a Southern gentility.

234

about food and love and getting together over a meal, and the couple wanted to send the same warm message in their own home.

They teamed up with architects Rick Spitzmiller and Robert Norris to design a classic nineteenth-century-style farmhouse faced in clapboard and fieldstone, and we furnished it with traditional pieces used in a casual way. Both the de Gournay wallpaper in the dining room and the old-fashioned print on the curtains in the living room have the kind of charm that is timeless. You're not sure if the house was decorated in 1910 or 2010, and that's the feeling we wanted.

The family room is open to the kitchen, and it's a real chef's kitchen. The family loves to cook and there's room for lots of friends to be in there with them, chopping and cooking. You wouldn't believe the meals that have come out of this kitchen. There's a big trestle table where everyone can sit down and eat right there, if they want to. Or they can move outside and sit at the table on the adjacent porch. We made sure there were plenty of places to eat and entertain in this house.

And then there's the Barn, made of vintage wood salvaged from various barns and reassembled in a new way. Now it houses a restaurant and the cooking school and a wine cellar. Kreis had a vision of how it should look and I helped her achieve it, adding a few ideas of my own. When our daughter, Alexandra, turned sixteen, John and I took her to Paris and we stayed at the Ritz. In the middle of the restaurant was a huge living tree. There was something utterly magical about it, and I never forgot it. So I re-created it in the Barn, as the final touch in this rustic setting, for the Beall family, who built this inspiring place that so many people love.

I like the way a chest anchors a space, and this Biedermeier piece was the perfect size for this odd-shaped spot next to the staircase. The clients had a lovely collection of silver objects, and I grouped them on top. The de Gournay wallpaper somehow opens up the room and makes you feel as if you're looking at the sky.

The first thing you see as you walk in the front door is the dining table from Ainsworth-Noah, which gets a lot of use because Sam and Mary Celeste are always inviting people over to their house. It's surrounded by tall chairs slipcovered in slubby linen, with a smart little pleat to finish the skirt. The slipcovers give the dining room a softer look, and they blend right in with the ivory shades in the Oushak rug.

238

The afternoon sunlight brings out the honey-colored tones of a Biedermeier chest in a corner of the living room. The curtain fabric picks up the honey color and adds a muted blue-green hue to the palette, the kind of color that looks as if it has already faded a bit. And the pattern seems a little old-fashioned, which contributes to the sense that the room has been here for years.

An antique caned chair, a wicker basket, a sisal rug—each adds another texture that enriches the way you experience the room. Texture attracts the eye. It adds another layer. You can almost feel what that cane would be like to the touch. Then there's the smooth, polished wood of the chest. On top, I created an arrangement of objects that follows the basic rule of something high, something medium, and something low. And it's layered, for depth. The curtain fabric is Chevalier by Zimmer + Rohde. The large vessel on the floor is Chinese and was used to hold wine.

The lime-washed oak paneling in the living room was milled from trees cut down on the property. It adds so much warmth and also gives the room a feeling of age. The upholstered furniture Nancy Corzine's Atherton sofas and Rose Tarlow's Regency sabreleg chairs—are all done in tones of beige, cream, and camel. Then the tufted leather chair adds a deep, rich caramel. It's old and beautiful, with its own personality. Rose Tarlow's Windsor coffee table is a bit unusual. Steps pull out on each side—more room for hors d'oeuvres and wine glasses, if needed.

243

This group of furnishings has a well-traveled air. A Biedermeier armchair mixes with Rose Tarlow's crackled lacquer K'ang Hsi coffee table, a Coromandel screen, and a Chippendale armchair from Dennis & Leen. I'll often upholster a sofa in two fabrics to add another layer of texture, as I did here. John Saladino's Tuscan sofa has linen on the frame and a strié velvet on the cushions, in the same blue-green color seen in the curtains. None of the picture frames match in the collection of drawings, but they're aligned in a way that makes them feel like a unit. And then the round vintage mirror breaks out of the rectangle and energizes the whole group.

244

It was quite an elaborate process to turn the rift-sawn white-oak paneling in the library that lovely shade of greige. And it involved several techniques—the wood was stained, limed, and glazed.

Look at the craftsmanship on this bookcase. I particularly like the way the shelves are designed. That ladder of wood strips on each side makes it easy to move them, and it's exceptionally sturdy. Paneled doors below open at the touch of a finger.

This may be the only farmhouse in Tennessee with tiger-stripe velvet chairs in the library. That Tiger Lino fabric, from Old World Weavers, upholsters two slightly different antique chairs, pulled up to a desk that was made around 1900 for the Banque de France. A vintage coffee table is decorated with a Greek-key design, which I picked up and used as a trim on my Emory sofa for Hickory Chair. The Paris wing chair by Scalamandré is upholstered in charcoal-gray mohair velvet by Rogers & Goffigon.

249

A rough slab of wood, made into a table, strikes a rustic note in the family room. This large, light-filled space, open to the kitchen, is the heart of the house.

OPPOSITE: Everyone wants to be near the kitchen, so a lot of family life happens in this room. That vintage table in the corner is a good place for doing homework or paying bills. The kids can pull up a stool and spread out their paper and crayons on the rough wood table. Nothing they could do can hurt it. The floor is made of wide oak planks and the rug was handwoven by Lyn Sterling Montague.

FOLLOWING SPREAD: The sitting area functions as a second living room. The stones for the fireplace were collected on the grounds. Rough-hewn beams and board-and-batten walls make it feel like a farmhouse. The furniture is upholstered in sturdy, family-friendly linen in tones of cream and beige. All the color is in the Robert Kime fabric on the curtains. It has a handmade look, and the vibrant pattern adds more life to the space.

RIGHT: I've seen as many as twelve people chopping, prepping, cooking, and cleaning in this kitchen. Miraculously, they don't even seem to get in one another's way. The cabinets are made from white oak and the countertops are black granite, honed instead of polished for a more natural look. It can take a beating and still look great. A rolling cart functions as a movable island and can go where it's needed. The gooseneck Perrin & Rowe faucet is available through Rohl. The Madigan stools are by Hickory Chair.

FOLLOWING PAGES: Even though this is a professional kitchen, there are still a few rustic notes. LEFT: A collection of old breadboards is displayed on one wall. Copper pots hang over a range by Jade. The backsplash is made of Gramercy Park tile by Walker Zanger. RIGHT: We designed a cozy banquette for this breakfast area. I like the contrast between the dark trestle table and the light Windsor chairs. The painting is by Ira Yeager.

ABOVE: The pantry, between the kitchen and the dining room, becomes an elegant black-lacquered bar area during a party. The mirrored backsplash seems to double the space and adds a glamorous touch. OPPOSITE: In the mudroom, vintage metal lockers make it easy to organize everyone's belongings.

FOLLOWING SPREAD: The porch is right off the kitchen, and that beat-up wooden table is the scene of many meals. One of the carpenters built the hanging swing, and artisans at the Bennett Galleries made the rustic log chairs. The outdoor Valencia rug is from Restoration Hardware.

The
Barn

PEARS

The idea behind Blackberry Farm is not only to come and enjoy yourself, but also to reconnect with the land. Everyone is encouraged to take part in any and all farm activities, and the center of all the action is the Barn. Here, gourmet meals featuring heirloom vegetables grown in the garden, home-cured charcuterie, and artisanal cheeses are served. And guest chefs share their techniques at the cooking school.

The beauty of an old barn is in the weathered wood and the big, lofty spaces. Kreis Beall wanted to preserve that feeling in the Barn, which houses the restaurant. Huge iron chandeliers light the entrance hall. To the left is the open kitchen. And to the right is my tree, inspired by the one I saw at the Ritz hotel in Paris. Here, I just walked out into the fields, pointed at a tree, and they dug it up and planted it in a pot for me. It makes you feel close to nature, even when you're inside.

264

Under the gambrel roof is a lounge area, with comfortable, casual furniture. You can sit down and have a drink and look out at the view. The linen slipcovers on the wicker chairs by the round tables tie in the back, on two sides. Cooking demonstrations take place at that huge island on the right. And in a whimsical moment, I hung antique weathered doors on top of the old barn wood. It adds another layer of texture.

266

RIGHT: The island in the
demonstration kitchen is
beautifully made. I like the
stainless-steel details on the
cabinet doors and the shelves.
The countertop is made of
limestone, and the glazed tile
on the backsplash picks up the
same soft color. I couldn't resist
the tree trunk tables. Obviously,
taking a class at this cooking
school is going to be fun.

FOLLOWING PAGES: Attention
to detail is a constant throughout
the Barn. LEFT: We designed
an entire room around the
Bealls' collection of antique
silver and crystal. The doors
have glass panes, so it can be
appreciated even when it's not
in use. RIGHT: In the restaurant,
the chairs are distinctively
shaped and comfortably
upholstered, so you can sit
happily for hours. The painting
is by Thrush Holmes.

Blackberry Farm is renowned for their exceptional collection of wines, and this might be the most exceptional place in which to drink them. A table runs the length of the wine cellar, which doubles as a tasting room—and the site of some splendid dinners. On either side, you can see through the windows to the wine racks. There's something fabulous about the contrast of fine silver and crystal against all that rough iron and stone.

ORGANIC

When our best friends from Indiana, Suzie and Fred Fehsenfeld, asked me to do a house for them in Africa, I knew it would be an adventure. There was only one problem. I'm not that adventurous. In fact, I'm scared of everything—snakes, wild animals, bugs. This was going to take me way out of my comfort zone, but I decided it was an opportunity I couldn't miss.

We sketched out the idea on a napkin—four separate cottages, with rounded walls and thatched roofs reminiscent of a traditional Kenyan village. One cottage for the kitchen, two for the bedrooms, and one for living, dining, and entertaining that would be totally open to the view . . . and to the animals. Really? What if an elephant walked right in? The whole concept was making me a little nervous, but that's the way people in these parts live. We were building the compound on the grounds of the Sirikoi game lodge, owned by the Fehsenfelds' good friends, Willie and Sue Roberts. (They also own the log cabin on Mount Kenya where Prince William proposed to Kate Middleton.) All of these properties are part of the Lewa Wildlife Conservancy, and our friends, like Willie and Sue, are completely committed to that cause.

A local architect, Barnaby Ghaui, took our rough sketch and made it fact. The way they build out here is very organic. They make smart use of indigenous materials.

Mirror, metal, horn, wood, and rock—texture tells a story. The walls of the cottages are
simple white plaster, and then Willie Roberts picked out just the right piece of wood and
made the mantel. I brought the lamp from Atlanta. It adds a warm, homey touch.

The distinctive wood columns that support the enormous palm-thatch roof were cut from fallen trees, and the placement was figured out on site. When they were ready to pitch the roof, I asked that it be a foot taller, to make the space feel even more airy. And I wanted the poured cement floor to be very simple, without the patterns they often add, so it felt more like bare earth.

I bought the major pieces of furniture—beds, sofas, chairs, tables—here in Atlanta and had it all packed into a container and shipped to Africa. Not everything was new—mixed in with the contemporary pieces were a few English antiques. I wanted the rooms to have a sense of history. And for that *Out of Africa* look I love, you need a little old-fashioned chintz. Then my associate, Keith Arnold, and I went back to Kenya and searched through local shops for accessories like beadwork, carved wooden stools, and handwoven textiles that would convey the flavor of the place. We had a lot of fun wandering through an outdoor crafts market in Karen, buying all sorts of baskets, big wooden bowls, and Kuba cloth.

Certain conventions fell aside. It just didn't seem appropriate to build closets into those beautiful round walls, so we had Gary McIntyre, who owns the East African Canvas Company, make canvas wardrobes with a flap that can be rolled up or down. They look like something you would use on a safari. Gary also made our luggage racks and the fabulous director's chairs, in leather for a touch of class. I love that kind of mix—like fine silver on a rough wooden table. The elegance is more striking because you see it against the natural elements.

The landscape is vast and overpowering. Vistas seem to go on forever, without any sign of civilization. In the wilds of Africa, it's easy to feel as if you're the only person on earth.

I love the drama of that soaring roof. You'll never guess what the chandelier is made of, so I'll tell you—ostrich eggs! This is the largest cottage, designed for socializing. Its centerpiece is a big wooden table, where you can dine or work.

OPPOSITE: I found the large wooden table at B. D. Jeffries in Atlanta and paired it with director's chairs made by the East African Canvas Company and an antique English bench covered in crewelwork. The bench reminds me of the kind of furniture the British settlers would have shipped out from England to make their East African coffee plantations feel more like home. Artist Sue Fusco made the fanciful chandelier.

FOLLOWING SPREAD: At night, the grounds are lit by lanterns. Made of natural materials, the four thatched-roof cottages (and a garage) seem to blend into the landscape.

The patio is sheltered by the roof and completely open on three sides, which makes it a great spot to sit and watch the wildlife. Most animals stay outside, but the monkeys are very mischievous. You have to be careful about what you leave out overnight because they have no qualms about coming in and snatching whatever they like. The furniture out here can stand up to the elements. A pair of wicker sofas from South of Market flanks a chunky wooden coffee table that we found at the outdoor market in Karen. The bar to the left comes in handy during a large party.

PREVIOUS SPREAD: There are two main seating areas in the large cottage, each anchored by a fireplace. The furniture is simple and tailored—two Eugenie sofas by Verellen slipcovered in natural linen, two Gunnison chairs from Hickory Chair in brown leather, and a Cate slipper chair by Victoria Hagan with a band of orange around the bottom, to pick up the color in the throw pillows. If the resident cheetah—an orphaned cub rescued by Willie and Sue Roberts—is not nearby, there are pillows covered in a cheetah print by Rose Cumming. We framed a fragment of Kuba cloth and hung it over the mantel. Window openings are encased in raw wood. There's no glass, only a canvas shade and a screen that can zip shut. A trunk from Restoration Hardware doubles as a side table. The sisal rug is from Stark.

RIGHT: The second seating area picks up the orange accents with bright Jim Thompson pillows and a striped slipcover on my Inman ottoman for Hickory Chair. The sofa and chairs are by Verellen. The leather-topped coffee table is from Mrs. Howard. We found the beaded baskets at the outdoor market. They're beautifully made and so unusual. Now I wish I had bought more of them!

Four prints by Peter Beard,
framed alike and grouped together,
form a focal point.

OPPOSITE: My Roswell sconce for Visual Comfort casts a little more light on the pictures. I am
entranced with Peter Beard's work. The way he manipulates images, writing all over them and creating
collages with various found materials, fascinates me. The cognac-colored leather on the director's
chair is beautiful and will become even more comfortable over time.

FOLLOWING SPREAD: A guest room is conveniently furnished with two beds that can be pulled
together or split apart. I did the room in warm, earthy colors, and then the Raoul Textiles linen on
the pillows brings in the glow of the afternoon sun. An animal print seemed appropriate in Africa so I
chose an antelope-patterned carpet by Helios. The leather club chair by the fireplace looks as if it was
transported from England, to give an expatriate a sense of home. And every guest room has to have a
desk. This one is from Restoration Hardware.

A small high-backed settee creates its own little nook by a window.

I found the beaded pillows and the beaded collars at the outdoor market in Karen. The bag slung over the settee is by Anna Trzebinski, who has a studio in Nairobi and makes the most beautiful clothes and accessories. I like the way the builders framed the windows with salvaged cedar, split open to reveal the grain. It looks like something that could have been done by George Nakashima.

ABOVE: Imagine how it must feel to sleep under that thatched roof. This guest room is a companion to the other, outfitted with the same kind of easily transportable furniture you might find on safari—a campaign desk by Bunny Williams and an upholstered camp chair from Hickory Chair. I also used the same antelope rug. Here, the two beds are pushed together. OPPOSITE: Fuchsia and orange are vibrant accents. You see those colors in the Raoul Textiles print—the same fabric I used in the other guest room, but in another colorway—and the suzani-covered pillow. The roll-up canvas wardrobe, with wooden shelves and leather buckles, was made by the East African Canvas Company, which also makes luxury tents and all sorts of accoutrements for the adventurous traveler.

OPPOSITE: I found a traditional African warrior's ceremonial dress, framed it, and hung it over my Asheworth campaign desk in the master bedroom. Then I tossed an Indian beaded throw over the bed—another idea of adornment. ABOVE: There are hints of Europe in the two chairs, covered in a traditional English chintz. I remember Meryl Streep leaning back against her chintz-covered chair in *Out of Africa* and this brings back that moment. I love the dichotomy of cozy English chintz under a rustic African roof.

ABOVE: The curved walls add a kind of gentleness to the house, and there's a rugged beauty to the natural materials. OPPOSITE: For some people, an outdoor shower is the definition of bliss. We designed the concrete wall, with its built-in bench, to look very organic. You feel as if you're at one with nature when you stand under a stream of water and gaze out at the view. Africa, with its infinite expanses and extraordinary wildlife, is glorious—and humbling. I'm very glad I came. And in this thatched-roof house, I feel as if I'm part of the substance and the spirit of the place.

ACKNOWLEDGMENTS

Thank you to my family, whose love and support has given me the freedom to be all I can be. I am grateful to my mother and father, who inspire me every day and have always encouraged me to keep my spirit and be true to myself.

Thank you to every member of my fabulous team, whose dedication and spirit make Suzanne Kasler Interiors the best place to go to work every day. I am particularly grateful to Keith Arnold for always being there for me. Special thanks to Julie Bowen, Karen Orr, and Dennis Hunt.

One of the most rewarding aspects of my work is collaborating with the most talented architects. I can't thank them enough for all they contribute to our work.

Thanks to the amazing contractors, artisans, and workrooms who always come through for us and without whom I could not accomplish as much. I especially want to thank Willard Pitt, my curtain maker, and Steve Cyr, who makes our installations happen.

To all the editors who have supported me and allowed my projects to grace their pages. To Margaret Russell, for believing in me and bringing my career to new heights, and for her friendship.

My sincere thanks to Charles Miers, publisher of Rizzoli International Publications, for believing in me; to Sandy Gilbert, whose focus and enthusiasm kept me on track; to Catherine Kraft and Clinton Smith, whose attention to detail made this book possible.

My deepest gratitude to Christine Pittel, who always captures so beautifully in words my voice and my passion for design.

To Jill Cohen, whose friendship, positive attitude, and guidance means so much to me.

Special thanks also go to Doug Turshen and David Huang for their amazing ability to translate my work into a beautiful book reflecting my own style.

To my licensing partners and associates, Hickory Chair, Visual Comfort, Safavieh, Soicher-Marin, Lee Jofa, and Ballard, who encourage me to be the best I can be.

Special thanks to Keith Granet, who has not only become my friend but also expanded my horizons to encompass new people and places.

To my wonderful clients, who have made all this possible.

PHOTOGRAPHY

beall + thomas photography: pages 262 (top, left; middle row; bottom left and right), 264–265, 266–267, 268–269, 270–271, 272–273

Erica George Dines Photography: pages 11, 12 (top, middle and right; middle, left; bottom left and right), 15, 16–17, 18-19, 20, 23, 26–27, 28–29, 31, 32–33, 34 (top, left and right; bottom, left), 35, 36, 38–39, 40–41, 43, 45, 46–47, 49, 53, 54–55, 57, 58–59, 63, 68–69, 102, 105, 106–107, 109, 110–111, 112–113, 115, 116–117, 118–119, 120–121, 123, 126–127, 128–129, 131, 132–133, 230, 233, 234–235, 237, 238–239, 242–243, 244–245, 247, 248–249, 251, 252–253, 254–255, 256–257, 258–259, front and back covers

Elliott's Studio: page 12 (middle, right)

Pieter Estersohn Photography: pages 12 (middle), 24–25, 34 (bottom, right), 44, 50–51, 60–61, 62, 64–65, 66–67, 124–125, 130, 134–135, 240, 254–255, 260–261, 262 (top, right); courtesy of *Architectural Digest*

Miguel Flores-Vianna: pages 208, 211, 212–213, 215, 216–217, 218–219, 221, 222–223, 224–225, 226–227, 228–229; courtesy of *Veranda*

Thibault Jeanson: pages 176, 179, 181, 183, 184–185, 186–187, 188–189, 191, 192–193, 194–195, 196–197, 198–199, 201, 202–203, 204–205, 206–207, 274 (top, left and middle; bottom left and right), 277, 279, 281, 282–283, 284–285, 286–287, 288–289, 291, 292–293, 295, 296–297, 298–299, 300–301

Joel Kelly: page 12 (top, left)

Pamela Mougin: page 274 (top, right; middle, center), author's portrait on jacket flap

Simon Upton: pages 2, 5, 8, 70, 73, 75, 77, 78–79, 80–81, 82–83, 84–85, 87, 88–89, 90–91, 93, 94–95, 96–97, 98–99, 100–101, 136, 139, 141, 142–143, 145, 146–147, 149, 150–151, 152, 154–155, 157, 158–159, 160–161, 162, 164–165, 166–167, 168–169, 170–171, 172–173, 174–175

ARCHITECTURE

William T. Baker, Atlanta, Georgia: pages 12–69, 102–135

Barnaby Ghaui, Naivasha, Kenya: pages 274–301

Harrison Design Associates, Atlanta, Georgia: pages 176–207

Land Plus, Atlanta, Georgia: pages 12 (bottom right), 16–17, 66–67, 68–69, 132–133

Pak Heydt & Associates, Atlanta, Georgia (with Spitzmiller & Norris): pages 70–101

Bill Huey & Associates, Atlanta, Georgia: pages 208–229

Sound Beach Partners, Stamford, Connecticut: pages 136–175

Spitzmiller & Norris, Atlanta, Georgia: pages 70–101, 230–261

Studio Chan Architecture, New York, New York: pages 136–175

First published in the United States of America in 2013
by Rizzoli International Publications, Inc.
300 Park Avenue South
New York, New York 10010
www.rizzoliusa.com

2015 2016 2017 / 10 9 8 7 6 5 4

PRINTED IN CHINA

ISBN 13: 978-0-8478-4100-4

Library of Congress Control Number: 2013939436

Project Editor: Sandra Gilbert
Production: Maria Pia Gramaglia
Editorial assistance provided by Hilary Ney,
Rachel Selekman, and Elizabeth Smith
Art Direction: Doug Turshen with David Huang
Endpapers: Atelier Stripe by Suzanne Kasler for Lee Jofa